The Confidence Chronicles

7 Faith-Fueled Principles to Rebuild Your Identity, Heal Your Story and Rise Across the 8 Core Life Areas
(Includes Self-Work Exercises & Reflective Practices)

By CoWano Stanley

Copyright © 2024 by CoWano Stanley
All rights reserved. No part of this publication may be reproduced, distributed, or transmitted in any form or by any means, including photocopying, recording, or other electronic or mechanical methods, without the prior written permission of the publisher, except in the case of brief quotations embodied in critical reviews and specific other noncommercial uses permitted by copyright laws.

Title: The Confidence Chronicles
Subtitle: 7 Faith-Fueled Principles to Rebuild Your Identity, Heal Your Story and Rise Across the 8 Core Life Areas
Life Areas (Includes Self-Work Exercises & Reflective Practices)
Author: CoWano Stanley
ISBN: 979-8-9988282-9-4

Table of Contents

Professional Speaker Information	5
For Your Journey	7
Introduction	9
Chapter 1: Believe to Become: The Foundation of Self-Belief	11
Chapter 2: Bold Action: Moving Through Fear with Faith	19
Chapter 3: Own Your Voice: The Power of Speaking Up	27
Chapter 4: Resilience Reset: Bouncing Back with Confidence	33
Chapter 5: Purpose in Practice: Living with Intentional Confidence	39
Chapter 6: Alignment Over Approval: Thriving Authentically	45
Chapter 7: Whole-Life Confidence: Creating Balance in the 8 Core Areas	51
Conclusion	57
Your Next Steps	59
Personal Affirmation	60
Acknowledgement	61
Social Media Contact	62

Professional Speaker Information

CoWano Stanley is from El Dorado, AR, but she grew up in Minneapolis, MN. She now resides in Las Vegas, NV. At the age of twenty, one of the most remarkable events in her life was the birth of her son. As a single parent, she completed two master's degrees. At the early age of five, she always stated that she would be her boss. So, at the age of twenty-six, she started working in her own cleaning business.

CoWano left the corporate world in accounting in 2018. She became a full-time entrepreneur at 39 years of age. While raising her son, she went through difficult times. She began to experience a lack of confidence in herself due to several abusive relationships and challenges as a single parent. CoWano's goals were delayed due to a lack of confidence. She recognized that a change needed to happen. So, she learned how to reclaim & ignite her confidence daily & walk in it boldly. By going through the challenges, she found her passion to help others. So, CoWano started her coaching program & public speaking to teach women the tools on how to reclaim & increase their confidence caused by trauma & life circumstances.

CoWano is the author of five self-published books. She is also a Co-Author in 9 Anthology books, three of them with International Empowerment Speaker Dr. Cheryl Woods and World Leading Motivational Speaker Les Brown. CoWano has been a featured speaker on stage with Dr. Cheryl Woods & Les Brown at You Are Enough & Dare to Rise Above Mediocrity

Virtual Conference and SpeakerCon Conference. She has also been a featured speaker on stages of Taurea Vision Avant (New Year New You Conference), JJ Conway (Women Building Wealth Together Conference), Elyshia Brooks (Bigger Bolder You Conference), Dr. Jennifer Harris (I Declare Summit), Angie Renee (Preserve and Inspire Conference) & Grace Quarshie (Women Who Make a Difference Conference in Africa). She has also done a workshop at the 36th Annual Executive Women in Texas Government (EWTG). She was featured in several magazines such as the Urban CEO Network (2X), Courageous Women, Speakers, Authors All-Star (2X), and Increase Business & Life. She has been seen on US National Times, Making Headline News, Roku, Amazon Fire TV, WWDBTV, Fox News, Small Business Online Network, and interviewed on the Ambitious Women Crowned TV Show.

    CoWano will continue to speak and coach women to increase and rebuild their confidence due to setbacks and life challenges.

To receive your FREE eBook access, go to
www.myconfidenceiskey.com.

For Your Journey

As you enter these pages, I pray you feel strength rising, clarity returning, and confidence awakening within you.

This book was written for women who have carried much, survived much, and deserve to rise again.

Let every chapter remind you:
God has not forgotten you.
Your story is not over.
And everything you've walked through has prepared you for where you are going.

Introduction

Confidence doesn't begin with the applause of others; it begins with the whisper of God reminding you who you are. I didn't always have confidence. In fact, for many years, I wore a mask that said "strong" on the outside but hid a heart full of insecurity, fear, and doubt. Like many women, I showed up for everyone else: family, work, ministry, but somewhere along the way, I stopped showing up for myself. I forgot what it felt like to trust my voice, to move boldly, or to believe I was worthy of the life I truly desired. What I've learned on this journey is that confidence is not about being perfect, loud, or polished. True confidence is rooted in knowing who you are in God and embracing that truth, even when life tries to convince you otherwise.

This book was born out of that revelation. *The Confidence Chronicles* is not just another motivational guide. It's a journey. A collection of God-inspired principles and real-life strategies that helped me and countless other women rise from discouragement, stagnation, and survival mode to a place of thriving in purpose, peace, and power.

You see, confidence isn't meant to stay in just one part of your life. When it's real, it flows into everything: how you parent, how you pursue your purpose, how you handle your finances, nurture your health, love others, speak up, and show up. That's why this book is focused on helping you grow confidence in the 8 Core Areas of Life:

1. Faith (Spiritual Life)
2. Family
3. Finances
4. Fitness (Health & Wellness)
5. Field (Career or Business)
6. Friendships
7. Fun (Joy & Recreation)
8. Fulfillment (Personal Growth)

Each chapter will walk you through a transformational confidence principle rooted in scripture, tested through experience, and designed to activate a breakthrough in these life areas.

You don't need to have it all figured out to start. You just need a willingness to believe again and to learn. To invite God into the places where your confidence has been shaken. And from there, your healing, rising, and thriving can begin.

I pray that as you read, you don't just gain information, you gain transformation. May this book remind you that you were never meant to shrink, settle, or stand in the shadows. You were created to rise, lead, and shine, with unshakable confidence.

Let's begin this journey together.

With grace and boldness,

CoWano Stanley

Chapter 1: Believe to Become: The Foundation of Self-Belief

Before you can step into your next level, you must believe that you belong there. Confidence doesn't begin with doing; it begins with believing, believing that you are worthy, that you are chosen, that God didn't make a mistake when He made you.

In a world full of noise, it's easy to lose sight of who you are. But self-belief is the quiet power that reminds you: *"I am capable. I am called. I am becoming."* This chapter is your invitation to silence doubt and root yourself in truth. What you believe about yourself determines what you allow yourself to become.

Identity Over Insecurity

You were not created by accident, and your identity is not up for negotiation. From the very beginning, God spoke purpose over your life. Before anyone had an opinion, before trauma left a scar, before doubt ever whispered, "you're not enough," you were already enough in Him. But life has a way of making us forget.

The voices of others, our mistakes, and painful experiences can cloud the truth of who we are. Maybe you were overlooked, rejected, or told to play small to keep the peace. Over time, these moments shape mindsets, and mindsets shape identity. Here's the truth:

- You are not your past.
- You are not your pain.
- You are not what they said about you.

You are who God says you are.

Story

I remember a season in my life when I felt completely invisible. I was working hard, trying to prove myself at work and in my relationships, but no matter what I did, it never felt like enough. I heard the words, "You're too much" or "You'll never make it" so often that I started to believe them. I doubted myself, my abilities, and even my purpose.

One morning, after yet another discouraging setback, I decided to stop trying to prove my worth to everyone else and started speaking truth about my life instead. I wrote down scriptures about my identity and read them out loud: "I am fearfully and wonderfully made. I am God's workmanship. I am loved and called." At first, it felt strange and even silly. I didn't feel different, but I kept speaking the words daily.

Over time, I began to notice subtle changes. I started taking bold steps in my career and personal life without waiting for approval. Doors began opening, opportunities I never imagined appeared, and I felt a quiet strength growing inside me. That's when I realized that confidence isn't about what others see, but rather about what you believe about yourself and where you anchor that belief.

Replacing lies with truth

Reclaiming your God-given identity starts by recognizing the lies you've believed. Some lies are deeply rooted and feel like facts because you've rehearsed them for years. Confidence grows when truth replaces lies.

Common identity lies and God's truth:
- **Lie:** "I'm not good enough."
  Truth: You are fearfully and wonderfully made. (Psalm 139:14)
- **Lie:** "I always mess things up."
  Truth: You are God's workmanship, created for good works. (Ephesians 2:10)
- **Lie:** "I have to earn love and approval."
  Truth: You are already loved and accepted in Christ. (Romans 8:38-39)
- **Lie:** "I'll never change."
  Truth: You are a new creation in Christ. (2 Corinthians 5:17)

Speaking Truth Daily

You won't always feel confident right away, and that's okay. Confidence isn't a feeling; it's a decision. Choosing to believe God's word about you begins to shift your life. The more you speak truth, the more you live it.

Morning Affirmation:

"Today, I release every lie spoken over me. I embrace my identity as a daughter/son of God, loved, called, and confident."

Remember: You are not here to become someone else; you are here to become you fully. Confidence isn't found in perfection; it's found in remembering who you already are in Him.

Faith-Fueled Confidence

Confidence rooted in self alone will always waver. It rises and falls with mistakes, missed opportunities, and uncertainty. But when confidence flows from faith in God, it becomes steady, unshakable, and sacred. Faith-fueled confidence doesn't mean you never doubt; it means that even in fear, you know who to turn to.

Trusting God Strengthens Self-Belief

Too often, we treat God like a backup plan. Confidence built that way is fragile, like building a house on sand. Faith-fueled confidence begins with God, stays rooted in God, and draws strength from His promises, not your performance.

"Blessed is the one who trusts in the Lord, whose confidence is in Him." —Jeremiah 17:7 (NIV)

Your confidence isn't about how much you know or how many people believe in you; it's about how deeply you trust the One who never changes.

Anchoring your worth

If your worth depends on your title, relationships, bank account, or appearance, it will always be fragile. God's love and calling for your life never change. Worth is not a moving target. It was set by God when He formed you in the womb and called you *"very good."* (Genesis 1:31)

"God is within her, she will not fall; God will help her at break of day." —Psalm 46:5 (NIV)

When your worth comes from God, your confidence becomes unshakable. You no longer strive to prove yourself; you simply show up as the person God already approved.

Live in Faith-Fueled Confidence
- Surrender the need for control
- Lean into God's promises even when circumstances feel uncertain
- Speak the truth aloud when lies creep in

Declaration:
"I no longer build my worth on things that fade. My confidence is rooted in Christ. I trust that what God placed in me is enough. I walk boldly, not because I have all the answers, but because I know the One who does."

Embrace Your Future Self

There's a version of you that God already sees strong, confident, free, and walking boldly in purpose. You don't become her/him by chasing perfection; you become her/him by choosing growth, healing, and believing the person God designed is already inside you.

Confidence doesn't wait for perfect timing; it creates it. Show up as if the breakthrough is already on the way, the door is opening, and the anointing rests on your life.

"She is clothed with strength and dignity; she can laugh at the days to come." —Proverbs 31:25 (NIV)

Release the Old You

To embrace your future self, release the old versions shaped by survival, silence, or shame. The version that tolerated less than you deserved. Thank her or him, then let her or him go. Becoming is obedience, not betrayal. Honor your past by using its lessons to fuel your future.

Becoming Requires:
- **Vision** — See yourself through God's eyes
- **Faith** — Believe you are equipped for what's ahead
- **Action** — Take steps now to align with who you're becoming

Declaration:

"I am becoming the woman/man God designed me to be. I release the old and step into the new. I am worthy of the calling on my life, and I walk in bold expectation of what's to come."

Self-Work Journal Reflection:
What habits, beliefs, or identities do I need to release to become the woman/man I'm called to be?

_____
_____
_____
_____

_____

What does "her/him" look like: emotionally, spiritually, mentally, and confidently?

_____
_____
_____
_____

_____

What is one small decision I can make today that aligns with that?

_____
_____
_____
_____

_____

Chapter 2: Bold Action: Moving Through Fear with Faith

Taking bold action is never easy. It demands that we step beyond the familiar, confront our fears head-on, and trust in something greater than ourselves. Whether in our careers, personal development, or spiritual journeys, the path to breakthrough is rarely smooth, but it is always worth it. I remember the moment I decided to leave my corporate accounting career to start my own business. Fear whispered that I wasn't ready, that I'd fail, and that I was risking stability. But something inside me, a quiet, unwavering faith, said, 'Step forward.' That one decision changed everything. I faced uncertainty, but with each step, I felt more aligned with my purpose and more confident in my ability to succeed.

In this chapter, we explore how faith becomes the bridge that carries us through fear. It's about choosing courage when uncertainty looms, and making decisions fueled not by doubt, but by belief in our potential and purpose. I've learned that bold action isn't reckless; it's intentional. It's the daily commitment to move forward, even when the next step isn't clear.

As you read, you'll discover real stories and practical insights designed to empower you to break free from hesitation, rewrite your narrative, and create momentum in every area of your life. Career shifts, personal growth breakthroughs, and spiritual awakenings all begin when you embrace boldness rooted in faith. Get ready to lean into your power and transform fear into fuel for your journey. Your breakthrough awaits.

Embracing Courage: How Faith Transforms Fear into Opportunity

Fear is one of the most natural emotions we experience, yet it often stands in the way of our greatest potential. It whispers doubts, paints worst-case scenarios, and urges us to retreat into comfort zones. But what if fear isn't the enemy? What if it's a signal pointing toward growth? When we choose to embrace courage, we begin to see fear not as a wall but as a gateway. I once had the opportunity to speak at my first conference, but my fear of public speaking almost held me back. I was terrified, imagining everything that could go wrong. Yet I chose faith over fear. I prepared, prayed, and stepped onto that stage. The experience not only boosted my confidence but also opened doors I had never imagined. Faith becomes the lens through which fear shifts from a paralyzing force into a powerful catalyst for change. Faith isn't about ignoring fear or pretending it doesn't exist; it's about trusting that on the other side of fear lies opportunity, healing, and transformation.

Imagine the moments in your life when you felt afraid but decided to act anyway. Maybe it was starting a new job, having a difficult conversation, or pursuing a dream that seemed impossible. Those moments are the true markers of courage. They remind us that faith and fear can coexist, but faith must be the louder voice. By leaning into courage and faith, you build resilience. You develop a new mindset that sees setbacks as lessons and challenges as invitations to rise higher. This shift changes everything; it empowers you to step forward boldly, knowing that fear is simply a sign you're on the brink of something meaningful.

Stepping Forward: Unlocking Breakthroughs in Career, Growth, and Spirit

Taking the first step toward change can feel like standing at the edge of a vast unknown. But every breakthrough, no matter how big or small, begins with movement. Stepping forward requires intention, vulnerability, and a deep belief that your best self is waiting on the other side. When I first applied for a role that seemed beyond my reach, doubt crept in. 'I'm not qualified enough,' I thought. But I reminded myself of the skills I had built and trusted the process. I applied, and though I was nervous during the interview, I eventually landed the position. That step forward not only advanced my career but also taught me that growth requires moving despite fear.

In your career, stepping forward might mean pursuing a new opportunity, asking for a raise, or leaving a role that no longer serves your purpose. In personal growth, it could be setting boundaries, seeking help, or committing to habits that nurture your wellbeing. Spiritually, stepping forward often calls us to deepen our connection to something greater, to listen more closely to our intuition, and align our actions with our core values.

Each step forward is an act of courage and self-love. It breaks the cycle of stagnation and opens doors to new possibilities. Sometimes progress comes in leaps; other times, it's slow and steady. But every step carries you closer to the life you're meant to live. Remember, breakthroughs don't always come with fanfare. Often, they are quiet victories: the decision to keep going, the choice to believe in yourself when no one else does, or the simple act of trusting your journey. As you step forward, you unlock the potential within you to thrive in your career, expand your personal growth, and deepen your spiritual life.

Self-Work Exercise 1: Identify and Reframe Fear

- Write down three fears currently holding you back.

  _____

  _____

  _____

  _____

- For each fear, ask yourself: *What opportunity might be hidden behind this fear?*

  _____

  _____

  _____

  _____

- Write a faith-based affirmation to counter each fear (e.g., "I trust that this challenge will help me grow").

_____
_____
_____
_____

Self-Reflection Questions:

When was the last time you acted despite fear? What was the outcome?

_____
_____
_____
_____

_____

How can you remind yourself daily that faith is stronger than fear?

_____
_____
_____
_____

Self-Work Exercise 2: Take Your Next Step
- Choose one area of your life (career, personal growth, or spiritual) where you feel stuck.

- Write down one small, specific step you can take this week to move forward in that area.
- Set a date and time to take this step and hold yourself accountable.

Self-Reflection Questions:

What feelings come up when you think about taking this step? Fear? Excitement? Both?

_____

_____

_____

How can you support yourself emotionally and spiritually as you move forward?

_____

_____

_____

Who in your life can you lean on for encouragement or accountability?

_____

_____

_____

_____

_____

Chapter 3: Own Your Voice: The Power of Speaking Up

There comes a moment in every woman's journey when silence is no longer an option, when the need to be heard becomes greater than the fear of being misunderstood. I've lived through that moment more than once. For years, I silenced myself to keep the peace, avoid conflict, or simply because I doubted whether my voice even mattered.

I remember one early morning at work, sitting in a meeting as decisions were being made that could have negatively impacted my team. My hands were clenched in my lap, and my stomach twisted with anxiety. I kept thinking, "Maybe it's better if I stay quiet. Maybe no one will notice if I don't say anything." But as the discussion continued, I felt my confidence slipping. Finally, I raised my voice, shaking at first. I shared my perspective clearly and honestly. The room went silent. And then slowly others began nodding, building on my ideas. That day, I realized that owning your voice isn't about perfection; it's about courage, truth, and authenticity.

Owning your voice doesn't mean you always have the perfect words. It means permitting yourself to express what's real, what's true, and what's necessary. Whether it's in a relationship, at work, in your community, or even in front of a mirror, speaking up is a radical act of self-love and self-respect. It's choosing to advocate for your needs, values, and dreams even when your voice shakes.

Breaking Silence: Reclaiming Confidence Through Authentic Expression

There was a time when I thought staying silent was safer. I believed that if I didn't rock the boat, ask for too much, or challenge what didn't feel right, I'd be accepted or at least protected. But what I didn't realize was that holding my voice back was shrinking my confidence, silencing my identity, and disconnecting me from who I truly was.

I remember a personal moment with my family. I disagreed with the financial decision they were making. I kept quiet, thinking that speaking up would cause tension. Weeks later, the choice backfired, creating unnecessary stress and frustration. The regret was heavy. Eventually, I found the courage to speak up honestly, respectfully, and clearly. Not only was the issue resolved, but my relationships were strengthened, and I felt a weight lifted from my heart. That's when I truly understood silence may seem safer, but it comes at a cost. Real peace comes from authenticity, from expressing your truth, not avoiding conflict.

Many of us have been conditioned to believe that silence equals strength, that being agreeable, quiet, or "easy to manage" is the right way to move through the world. But suppressing your voice doesn't create peace; it creates internal conflict. Confidence grows the moment you choose to express yourself authentically. Your voice is not just about what you say, it's about how you live, how you show up, and how you allow others to experience the real you. I've seen this play out countless times in my life. Speaking up at work earned me a promotion. Speaking up in relationships deepened bonds I once thought were too fragile to survive honest conversation. And speaking up for myself in personal decisions transformed my sense of self-worth.

Speaking with authenticity doesn't require perfection; it requires presence. It means honoring your thoughts, feelings, and experiences enough to give them a voice. When you do this, you also permit others to do the same. Your voice has the power to heal, to lead, and to ignite. It's time to stop shrinking, stop hiding, and start standing in your truth. This is your moment to own your voice fully, boldly, unapologetically. Every word you speak, every truth you share, is a step toward the confident, powerful woman you were always meant to be.

Self-Reflection Questions:
Where in your life have you been silent out of fear or discomfort?

_____

_____

_____

_____

What truth have you been holding back that needs to be spoken, even just to yourself?

_____

_____

_____

How would your confidence shift if you allowed yourself to be fully heard?

Self-Action Exercise:
- Write a letter to yourself, from your most authentic, confident voice.
- In the letter, affirm your right to speak up, to be heard, and to be seen.
- Read it out loud to yourself in the mirror. Notice how it feels to hear your voice express truth.

From Fear to Freedom: Speaking Your Truth with Boldness and Grace

Fear often stands between us and our voices. We worry about being judged, misunderstood, or rejected. We fear that if we speak up, we'll be labeled as "too much" or "not enough." I've felt that fear myself, the heavy knot in my stomach before saying something that mattered, the endless "what ifs" running through my mind. But over time, I've learned that my voice was never the problem; fear was simply trying to protect me from pain.

Growth doesn't happen in silence. It happens when we use our voice with intention, not to hurt, but to heal; not to control, but to connect. I remember a moment when I had to set a boundary with a close friend. My heart raced, and I worried about the consequences, but I chose to speak from a place of honesty and love. The conversation wasn't perfect, but it strengthened our relationship and reinforced my self-respect. That day, I understood that speaking your truth with boldness and grace is one of the most courageous things you can do.

Boldness doesn't mean shouting the loudest; it means speaking from a place of inner conviction, with clarity and love. Grace doesn't mean sugar-coating your truth; it means delivering it with empathy and strength. Freedom comes when you release the need to be perfect and choose to be real instead. Every time you speak up, whether it's setting a boundary, telling your story, asking for help, or advocating for yourself, you are declaring, "I matter." That declaration is the foundation of true confidence, and it is how freedom begins to flourish.

Self-Reflection Questions:
What is one area of your life where fear has muted your voice?
_____
_____

_____
What does freedom sound like for you? How would your tone, language, and presence shift if you believed your voice was fully

worthy?

_____

_____

_____

_____

Self-Action Exercise:

- Make a list of three situations where you'd like to speak up more boldly in your personal, professional, or spiritual life.
- For each, write one empowering sentence you could say that reflects your truth.
- Practice saying them aloud until they feel natural in your body and spirit.

Your voice is a divine gift, a tool for connection, truth, and transformation. When you own it, you reclaim parts of yourself that were hidden or dismissed. Don't wait for permission to be heard. Speak. Not with fear, but with faith. Not with apology, but with authenticity. Because your voice, yes, your voice was meant to be a force of freedom, healing, and bold, beautiful confidence.

Chapter 4: Resilience Reset: Bouncing Back with Confidence

There was a time in my life when I didn't recognize the woman in the mirror. Behind her eyes was exhaustion not just from long days and sleepless nights, but from silently carrying the weight of broken dreams, lost confidence, and a heart bruised by life's battles. I was a single mom, juggling school, motherhood, and surviving domestic violence & financial struggles. I smiled at my child while quietly questioning if I'd ever feel whole again. What I know now, what life has taught me through every heartbreak, every setback, and every quiet triumph, is this: resilience is not about being unbreakable. It's about choosing to rebuild, even when everything in you want to give up. It's the decision to rise not perfectly, not painlessly, but powerfully, and with purpose.

This chapter is for the woman/man who has been knocked down by life and wonders if you anything left to give. This is your reset, not just in mindset, but in identity. You are not defined by what happened to you, but by what rises within you. Resilience and confidence walk hand in hand. When one is shaken, the other can still carry you forward if you're willing to trust yourself again.

We're going to explore how to reset after the fall, rebuild your belief in yourself, and step back into your power with boldness. Whether you're coming out of a toxic relationship, facing the aftershock of failure, or learning to live again after loss, this is your turning point. You don't have to have it all figured out. You just have to believe that your next chapter can be better than your last. I'm living proof that it can. Let's take this next step together confidently, courageously, and without apology.

From Wounds to Wisdom: Turning Pain into Power

There's a pain that doesn't leave a visible scar, yet it lives in your bones and whispers in your silence. I know that pain. For years, I carried the invisible wounds of domestic violence. The emotional manipulation, the fear, the constant feeling of walking on eggshells stripped me of my voice, my confidence, and my sense of safety.

There were nights I cried quietly so my child wouldn't hear. Days I smiled for the world while shrinking inside. I told myself, "Just keep going," all while wondering how much longer I could pretend to be okay. I stayed longer than I should have, not because I didn't know better, but because trauma convinces you that chaos is normal and your worth is negotiable.

One day, something shifted when I tried to take my own life. I heard my child's voice and saw a future I refused to sacrifice. I decided not just to leave, but to truly live. Leaving wasn't the end of the struggle; it was the beginning of my healing. I had to rebuild myself from the ground up, brick by painful brick.

Through prayer, therapy, journaling, and soul work, I began to see that my wounds carried wisdom. Every tear taught me something. Every scar told a story of survival. And every step toward healing gave me new power, my power not borrowed from anyone else, not dependent on approval, but rooted in truth, strength, and self-worth. Today, I don't see myself as broken. I see myself as rebuilt.

I remember one night, vividly sitting at the kitchen table with nothing but a notebook and a pen. I wrote out every fear, every regret, every "what if" that haunted me. I didn't know at the time that writing them down would be the first act of reclaiming my life. That night, I realized that the power to change my story had always been in my hands. That was my first step toward resilience, a step that eventually became a leap.

And that's what I want for you: to take what hurt you and let it shape you into someone even stronger, wiser, and more compassionate than before.

Action Steps: From Wounds to Wisdom
1. Acknowledge Your Pain: Write down what hurt you so you can face it instead of carrying it silently.
2. Reclaim Your Voice: Say or journal: *"This happened, but it will not define me."*
3. Find One Lesson: Turn your pain into wisdom by asking, *"What did this teach me about myself?"*
4. Take One Brave Step: Set a boundary, ask for help, or do one thing that moves you forward.
5. Celebrate Small Wins: Each day, note one moment you showed strength or resilience.

Self-Reflection

What wound in your life has tried to define you?
_____
_____

What wisdom can you now take from that experience?
_____
_____
_____

*Journal your thoughts for 10 minutes. Be honest. Be kind to yourself. This is not about judgment but of release. *

Self-Empowerment Exercise: Reclaim Your Power List

Take a moment and list 5 ways you've been strong even when you didn't feel like it. These could be small or large moments. Example:
- I got out of bed when I didn't want to.
- I asked for help.
- I protected my child.
- I started therapy.
- I walked away from a toxic situation.

Read your list out loud. Let yourself feel how powerful you already are.

The Healing Path to a Confident Comeback

Healing isn't a straight line; it's a sacred spiral. Some days, you feel like you're soaring; other days, the pain resurfaces as if to remind you it's still there. That's the truth of healing: it's layered, and it takes time. But with every step, you gain something new: clarity, compassion, and confidence.

Confidence didn't come from affirmations alone. It came from doing the work, facing the mirror, forgiving myself, and trusting God to guide me toward wholeness. I had to grieve who I used to be to make room for who I was becoming. I learned to speak life over myself again. I reminded myself that my past didn't cancel my purpose.

One of the most profound lessons I learned was this: healing happens when you stop hiding from your pain, your truth, and your power. When you show up fully, scars and all, you permit others to do the same.

Today, I coach women on this same path, not because I have it all figured out, but because I've been in the valley and made my way back. I walk with confidence, not because life is perfect, but because I've proven to myself that I'm resilient. That I can rise. That I have risen. And so can you. Your story is not over. What you've been through does not define you; it prepares you. You're allowed to grow beyond your pain. You're allowed to be joyful. You're allowed to be powerful. You're allowed to rise. Let this chapter mark your reset. Let this be the moment you stop surviving and start thriving. You are not broken, you are becoming.

Self-Reflection

What does a confident comeback look like for you?

_____

_____

Write a vision for who you are becoming. How do you speak? Show up? Carry yourself?

_____

_____

_____

_____

Self-Healing Exercise: "I Release, I Receive"

Fold a piece of paper in half.

On the left side, write the words:

I Release…

List what you're ready to let go of: fear, shame, guilt, self-doubt, trauma, old stories.

On the right side, write the words:

I Receive…

Now, list what you are ready to welcome in: peace, strength, confidence, clarity, and healthy love.

Take a deep breath. Tear the paper in half and keep the "I Receive" side somewhere visible as a reminder of your new chapter.

Chapter 5: Purpose in Practice: Living with Intentional Confidence

There was a time in my life when I mistook busy for purposeful. I filled my days with endless tasks, wore productivity like a badge of honor, and kept moving because stillness felt too close to pain. On the outside, I looked strong, ambitious, and put together. But on the inside, I was running on empty. I wasn't aligned. I was surviving, not truly living.

My confidence, though slowly being rebuilt after trauma, still lacked direction. I was piecing myself back together but hadn't yet discovered how to live on purpose, with purpose. It wasn't until I finally paused and asked myself, "What am I here for?" that everything began to shift. I had overcome heartbreak, survived abuse, rebuilt my life as a single mother, and launched both my career and calling. But something deeper was pulling at me, the desire to live intentionally. I wanted to wake up each day with clarity, joy, and courage, not just for myself, but for the people God had called me to impact.

This chapter is about that shift from existing to aligning, from healing to living, from merely reclaiming confidence to anchoring it in purpose. Because confidence without purpose can still leave you drifting. But when your confidence fuels your calling, your life becomes unstoppable. Living with intentional confidence means you no longer shrink to fit someone else's expectations. You no longer wait for permission to show up fully. Instead, you lead your life, your choices, and your relationships with intention. You choose to be present, bold, and unapologetically you not out of ego, but from a place of alignment with who God created you to be.

In this chapter, we'll explore what it looks like to put purpose into practice, not as a distant dream but as a daily lifestyle. I'll share how I learned to align my gifts with my goals, how I broke free from people-pleasing, and how I began showing up with clarity and confidence in everything from my business to my relationships.

Purpose is not just about doing big things; it's about doing the right things with heart, clarity, and conviction.

Aligning Your Actions with Your True Purpose

Living with intentional confidence begins when your daily actions reflect your true purpose. But what does it mean to live in alignment with your purpose? It means your choices, efforts, and mindset are all moving in the same direction that God designed for you.

For years, I felt caught in the whirlwind of responsibilities. I was doing "all the things" but still felt empty, disconnected from meaning. It wasn't until I created space for quiet reflection through prayer, journaling, and honest self-conversations that I began to sense the whisper of God's calling.

Purpose isn't about achieving one grand destination. It unfolds step by step. It's revealed in both milestones and the ordinary moments. God's plan isn't rushed. It's built through small, consistent acts of faith, courage, and obedience. When I started aligning my actions with my purpose, I realized it wasn't about chasing recognition or hustling for worthiness. It was about daily intentions rooted in faith. Instead of asking, "What will people think?" I began asking, "Does this honor who God created me to be?" That single shift in mindset built confidence that external circumstances could no longer shake.

A Personal Shift Toward Purpose

I'll never forget one particular morning during one of the hardest seasons of my life. I woke up exhausted, my mind racing with bills, responsibilities, and the weight of trying to hold everything together as a single mom and full-time entrepreneur. I remember sitting on the edge of my bed, tears in my eyes, tempted to crawl back under the covers and let the day swallow me. But instead of giving in, I grabbed my journal and forced myself to write one simple prayer: "God, give me strength for today." Then I wrote down one small intention: "I will not quit. I will show up with faith."

That moment didn't magically erase the struggle, but it gave me just enough courage to stand up, get dressed, and face the day with purpose. It taught me that intentional living doesn't always start with a grand vision. Sometimes it begins with a small, quiet decision to keep moving forward in faith. That was the day I realized purpose isn't only found in big milestones. It's built in the little choices we make daily to align our hearts with God's plan.

Self-Exercise: Discover Your Core Purpose
- Take out a journal or quiet space to reflect.
- Ask yourself:
    - What activities make me feel most alive?
    - When do I feel most connected to God's guidance?
    - What talents or gifts do I feel called to share?
    - How do I want to impact the lives of others?
- Write freely without judgment.
- Highlight recurring themes or feelings that emerge.
- Pray or meditate on these insights, asking God to clarify and strengthen your understanding.

Building Daily Habits That Reflect Confident Intentions

Intentional confidence isn't a one-time decision. It's a lifestyle sustained by daily habits. Think of your habits as the bricks building the foundation of your purpose-driven life. Every prayer, every act of kindness, every boundary you set, every moment of self-care is an expression of your confidence in God's plan. One powerful habit I built was starting each morning with gratitude and a clear intention: "Today, I will act with courage and kindness." This simple practice reframed my perspective, kept me focused on my purpose, and gave me the strength to handle challenges without losing myself.

I also learned the importance of saying "no" to things that drained me, even if they looked good on the surface. Every "no" to distraction became a "yes" to alignment. When your daily habits reflect your purpose, you stop living reactively and begin living proactively. You're no longer tossed by every storm; you're anchored.

Self-Exercise: Create Your Confidence Ritual
- Choose 2-3 small habits that connect you to your purpose and faith. Examples:
    - Morning prayer or meditation
    - Reading an inspiring passage or affirmation
    - Writing down one thing you're grateful for
    - Setting a daily intention aligned with your purpose
- Commit to practicing these habits every day for 21 days.
- Reflect weekly on how these habits influence your confidence and actions.
- Adjust or add new habits as your journey evolves.

Embracing God's Purpose for Your Life
Remember, your confidence is anchored in the truth that God created you intentionally and uniquely for a reason. As Jeremiah 29:11 reminds us:

"For I know the plans I have for you," declares the Lord, "plans to prosper you and not to harm you, plans to give you hope and a future."

Living with intentional confidence means trusting this promise and choosing to walk boldly, even when the path isn't fully clear. It's about daily surrender, releasing control, and leaning on God's wisdom while taking courageous steps forward in faith.

When you align your actions with your true purpose and cultivate habits rooted in prayer, gratitude, and intention, you begin to live a life that feels whole and powerful. Your confidence stops depending on external approval and instead rests on the unshakable foundation of knowing you are walking in God's calling with purpose.

And that's where your breakthrough lies, not in perfection, but in living with intentional confidence, step by step, day by day.

Chapter 6: Alignment Over Approval: Thriving Authentically

In a world that constantly whispers, "Fit in." Be liked. gain approval, it's easy to lose sight of who we are. The hunger for acceptance can feel like a compass guiding our choices, but if we follow it blindly, it will lead us away from our inner truth. This chapter is an invitation to pause, breathe, and rethink what it means to thrive not by the standards set by others, but by the quiet, powerful rhythm of your own heart.

Choosing alignment over approval is an act of courage. It means honoring your values, passions, and unique voice even when it feels uncomfortable or misunderstood. It's daring to show up fully, not as a reflection of someone else's expectations, but as an authentic expression of yourself. When you choose alignment, you unlock a freedom no external validation can provide. That freedom carries peace, purpose, and an unshakable confidence rooted in who God made you to be.

The Courage to Choose Yourself: Breaking Free from the Need for External Validation

From the time we were young, we're often taught without words that approval is the key to worth. Praise from parents, acceptance from friends, recognition from teachers, or bosses, all of it feeds the belief that we earn value by how others respond to us. But living for approval is like navigating with someone else's map; you'll always end up lost, frustrated, and empty. Choosing yourself takes courage. It means saying, "Even if no one claps for me, I'm still worthy." It means walking away from what doesn't align, even if it disappoints people you love. Most of all, it means realizing that your value isn't tied to anyone's opinion, it's rooted in God's truth. I know this firsthand. I spent years molding my words and actions to keep the peace, to please others, to avoid conflict. But every time I did, I felt smaller inside. It wasn't until I started honoring my voice and trusting that God placed it within me for a reason that confidence began to grow. The fear didn't disappear, but step by step, it loosened its grip.

A Real-Life Moment

One of my coaching clients, let's call her Monica, came to me struggling with a decision about her career. She was offered a promotion that everyone told her she "should" take, but deep down she knew it wasn't aligned with her passion or values. She said, "If I say no, people will think I'm ungrateful. If I say yes, I'll feel trapped."

Together, we unpacked her fear of disappointing others and centered on what God was placing in her heart. Eventually, Monica turned down the promotion. At first, her coworkers didn't understand. But months later, she stepped into a role that matched her calling and lit her up with joy. She told me, "Choosing alignment over approval felt scary, but now I finally feel free." That's the power of choosing yourself; it may cost you people's applause, but it gives you peace that applause can never buy.

Self-Exercise: The Approval Detox
- For one week, notice moments when you catch yourself seeking approval (on social media, in conversations, or in decisions).
- Journal these moments. Ask: *"Am I choosing this because it feels right, or because I want approval?"*
- Each day, practice saying one authentic statement aloud. Example: *"I choose my path, not theirs."*
- At the end of the week, reflect on how this shifted your confidence and peace.

Living True to Your Values: Unlocking Confidence Through Authentic Alignment

Your values are the compass that guides your life. They reveal what matters most about your priorities, your beliefs, your faith. Living true to your values creates integrity, clarity, and peace. But alignment takes courage. It means saying no to what doesn't serve your soul, even if others expect you to say yes. It's asking yourself daily: "Does this honor who I am?"

There were times I compromised my values just to avoid conflict or gain approval. Each time, I felt a little more disconnected from myself. But when I finally began making decisions rooted in my values, even when it meant someone else was disappointed, I discovered a new kind of strength. It wasn't about proving myself to others but honoring who God made me to be.

Self-Exercise: Clarifying Your Core Values
- Write down your **top 5 values** (examples: faith, honesty, family, independence, growth).
- Reflect on recent decisions. Which ones honored your values? Which didn't?
- Identify one area where you feel misaligned. What's one small step you can take to realign?
- Speak this affirmation daily: "I live with integrity and honor my true self."

God's Purpose for Your Life

God created you with intention and love, designed to walk a path only you can travel. Alignment is not about perfection; it's about living authentically, reflecting His truth in the world. When you choose alignment over approval, you become a light that guides others toward courage and freedom. As Ephesians 2:10 (NLT) reminds us:

"For we are God's masterpiece. He has created us anew in Christ Jesus, so we can do the good things He planned for us long ago."

And as Matthew 5:16 (NIV) says:

"Let your light shine before others, that they may see your good deeds and glorify your Father in heaven."

Final Reflection

Thriving authentically begins with a choice, the bold decision to align with God's purpose rather than people's approval. It requires faith, courage, and vulnerability, but it leads to joy, freedom, and unstoppable confidence. You are worthy. You are enough. And your most authentic self is waiting for you to say yes.

Chapter 7: Whole-Life Confidence: Creating Balance in the 8 Core Areas

Confidence isn't just about how you look when you walk into a room, speak on a stage, or share your story online. True, lasting confidence is built quietly, day by day, in the way you show up across every part of your life. It's not about perfection, it's about alignment. When your spiritual, emotional, physical, financial, relational, professional, personal, and recreational areas are nurtured with intention, confidence flows more naturally. You stop striving and start becoming.

Too often, we compartmentalize our lives, pouring into one area while neglecting another, leaving us feeling overwhelmed, disconnected, or incomplete. But God didn't design us to live in fragments. He created us as whole people, with dreams, needs, and gifts that stretch beyond any single title or role. Confidence grows when each area of your life speaks the same truth: I am enough, and I am becoming.

The Wholeness Within: Building Confidence Through Inner Alignment

Think of your life like a wheel with eight spokes. If one is neglected, the ride becomes bumpy. But when each one is cared for, your life moves with greater ease, grace, and momentum. I used to overcompensate in my professional life to avoid the emotional and spiritual gaps within me. On paper, I looked accomplished with degrees, career, and achievements. But inside,

I felt fractured, like I was living several disconnected lives. The turning point came when I realized God didn't call me to succeed in one area while silently suffering in the others. He called me to wholeness. And maybe you've been there, too. Maybe you've been the friend who looks strong on the outside but feels empty inside. Or the woman balancing motherhood, career, health issues, and relationships while quietly neglecting her own needs. Real confidence doesn't come from fixing everything at once. It comes from choosing to live truthfully and intentionally.

Self-Exercise: The Check-In Alignment

Take a quiet moment and rate each of the 8 core areas (Spiritual, Emotional, Physical, Financial, Relational, Professional, Personal, Recreational) on a scale of 1–10.

- Which areas feel strong and life-giving?
- Which ones feel neglected or draining?
- What would alignment look like in this area?

Choose your top 2–3 lowest areas to focus on. Write one small action step you can take this week.

💡 *Example: If your emotional confidence feels low, your step might be, "Schedule a session with a therapist, coach, or trusted mentor."*

Remember: Transformation doesn't happen overnight. But each intentional step creates momentum.

From Overwhelm to Overflow

So many women carry the silent burden of being everything to everyone. We juggle roles, responsibilities, and expectations often at the expense of our peace. The result? Overwhelm, burnout, and a whisper that says: "There's got to be more than this." That whisper isn't weak. It's wisdom. It's your soul asking for balance, not just to survive the day, but to start living from a place of overflow.

I remember a season when I wore "busy" like a badge of honor. I thought the more I did, the more worthy I'd be. But God showed me that constant busyness wasn't faithfulness, it was avoidance. I was pouring into everyone but myself. Eventually, I had nothing left to give, which also affected my health.
It wasn't until I slowed down, reset, and created margin that I began to live from overflow. Now, I align my days with what matters most because peace is more powerful than performance.

Self-Exercise: The Balance Blueprint

1. **List Your Priorities** → What truly matters to you in this season? Choose no more than 5.
2. **Audit Your Time** → For one week, track where your time goes.
3. **Compare & Adjust** → What can be delegated, delayed, or deleted?
4. **Build In Margin** → Schedule time for stillness, prayer, movement, fun, and rest.

5. **Daily Overflow Practice** → Each morning, ask: *"What do I need to feel full today?"*

God's Purpose for Wholeness

Psalm 139 reminds us: *"You are fearfully and wonderfully made."* That means every area of your life matters to Him. Balance is not about perfection or control; it's about surrendering your rhythm to God's design.

Jesus said in Matthew 11:28: *"Come to me, all who are weary, and I will give you rest."* Confidence doesn't grow in constant striving. It grows in wholeness, in knowing you are enough, and in walking with Him.

The 8 Core Areas of Whole-Life Confidence

Each of these areas is a vital part of your identity. When one is neglected, it can quietly drain your confidence. But when nurtured with love and intention, you feel whole, grounded in who you are, and confident in how you show up.

1. **Spiritual Confidence**

    Your relationship with God is your foundation. It grounds you in peace and guides your purpose.

    Self-Reflection: How often do I pause to connect with God and listen for His direction?

2. **Emotional Confidence**

    Resilience grows when you allow yourself to feel, heal, and manage your emotions with grace.

Self-Reflection: Do I give myself permission to feel and process my emotions in healthy ways?

3. **Physical Confidence**

   Your body is the vessel for your purpose. Caring for it is stewardship, not vanity.

   Self-Reflection: Am I treating my body as a partner in my purpose or neglecting it?

4. **Financial Confidence**

   Peace with money comes from wise stewardship, not striving. It creates freedom to focus on your calling.

   Self-Reflection: Am I managing my finances from fear, or from faith and wisdom?

5. **Relational Confidence**

   Your relationships shape how you give and receive love. Healthy boundaries and respect are key.

   Self-Reflection: Are my relationships nourishing me or draining me?

6. **Professional Confidence**

   Your work is an expression of your gifts and calling. Confidence grows when you know your value.

   Self-Reflection: Am I showing up in my work with excellence and authenticity?

7. **Personal Confidence**

   Beyond titles and roles, this is who you truly are. Confidence comes from embracing your uniqueness.

Self-Reflection: When was the last time I did something simply because it brought me joy?

8. **Recreational Confidence**

    Rest and play are not extras; they're essentials that fuel creativity, joy, and renewal.

    Self-Reflection: Do I regularly make time for fun and activities that make me feel alive?

Final Reflection: Living Whole

Whole life confidence is not a destination; it's a sacred rhythm. It's the courage to align with your truth and God's design, and the wisdom to release what drains you.

You don't have to "do it all." You just have to live whole. That's where your confidence becomes unshakable.

Conclusion: Your Confidence, Your Legacy

As you close this book, remember, confidence is not a fleeting feeling reserved for big moments; it is a lifelong journey, rooted in who you are at your core. The 7 Faith-Fueled Principles to Rebuild Your Identity, Heal Your Story, and Rise Across the 8 Core Life Areas you've explored are not just lessons to read; they are invitations to live boldly, love deeply, and thrive authentically in every season of life. True confidence grows when you embrace your whole self, spirit, emotions, body, relationships, work, and passions in alignment with God's unique design for you. It is not found in the approval of others, but in the courage to choose yourself, stand in your truth, and walk faithfully in your calling.

Yes, your journey toward confidence will include challenges. There will be seasons of doubt, but also breakthroughs of clarity. Through it all, hold fast to this truth: you are fearfully and wonderfully made, equipped with everything you need to rise, reclaim your power, and shine your light.

The 8 core areas of life are your canvas. When nurtured with intention and grace, they become the brushstrokes of a masterpiece of your confident, fulfilled, God-centered life. Now is your time. Step forward with boldness. Cultivate the confidence that transforms not only your world but also inspires others to rise with you. This is more than your story; it is your legacy. Live it with courage. Live it with joy. Live it confidently.

Your Next Step: A Call to Confident Action

Now that you've explored the principles and practices for building lasting confidence across all areas of your life, it's time to move from reading to doing. True confidence is developed through consistent, courageous action, no matter how small the step is.

Ask yourself:

- What is one choice I can make today that aligns with my values and moves me closer to my purpose?
- How can I nurture balance and alignment in the areas of my life that need attention?
- Who can I inspire or uplift with the confidence I am reclaiming?

Every step forward is a victory, every setback a lesson, and every day a fresh opportunity to live boldly and fully. Commit to this journey with grace and determination, knowing that your authentic confidence has the power to transform not just your life, but the lives of those around you.

To continue your journey, receive your **FREE eBook** at: www.myconfidenceiskey.com.

Personal Affirmation: I Am Confident, Whole, and Purpose-Driven

I am fearfully and wonderfully made, uniquely designed to shine.

I choose to honor all parts of myself and live with integrity.

I release the need for approval and embrace the courage to choose myself.

I walk in balance, aligned with God's purpose for my life.

My confidence grows daily as I step boldly into my calling.

I am enough, I am worthy, and I am becoming.

Acknowledgement

To everyone who preordered, supported, and believed in *The Confidence Chronicles*, thank you.

Your support means more than words can express. You didn't just invest in a book, you invested in a movement of healing, growth, and bold confidence.

I'm deeply grateful for your encouragement and belief in this message. I pray this book inspires you to live boldly, love deeply, and thrive fully.

With deep gratitude,

CoWano Stanley

Nancy Montgomery,	St Paul, MN
Gloria Abbott,	Brooklyn Center, MN
TaTika Taylor,	Minneapolis, MN
LaTonia Stanley,	Oakland, CA
Lynette Campbell,	Milwaukee, WI
Sonya Carter,	Accokeek, MD
Jennifer Levy,	Dallas, TX
Dexter Ansley,	Watsonville, CA

Social Media Follow

IG: startupwomenalliance

IG: loveme_coco

Linkedin: cowanostanley

FB: cowanococostanley

TikTok: cowanostanley

Twitter: cowanostanley

YouTube: cowanococostanley

Request CoWano Stanley to speak at your next Event/Conference

https://form.jotform.com/cstanley326/booking

www.ingramcontent.com/pod-product-compliance
Lightning Source LLC
Chambersburg PA
CBHW071231160426
43196CB00012B/2474